Learn Italian

A beginner's guide to learning basic Italian fast, including useful common words and phrases!

Table Of Contents

Introduction   iii

Chapter 1. Getting Started With The Italian
Language   1

Chapter 2. The Italian Alphabet   4

Chapter 3. Pronunciation Rules For Consonants 12

Chapter 4. Date, Time, And Numbers In Italian 28

Chapter 5. Italian Grammar Rules For Nouns   39

Chapter 6. An Introduction To Italian Articles   50

Chapter 7. Common Italian Phrases   55

Introduction

I want to thank you and congratulate you for downloading the book, *"Learn Italian"*.

This book contains helpful information about learning Italian. Italian is a fun and enjoyable language to learn, and due to its similarities with English, it's a great language to learn!

This book will teach you the basics of Italian, including common words and phrases, the alphabet, how to count, and proper pronunciation.

You will also learn when to use the different Italian articles, including when to use female articles, male articles, and their plural and singular versions.

With the information in this helpful book, you will be well on your way to mastering basic Italian, and have the ability to conduct basic communication in this amazing language!

Thanks again for downloading this book. I hope you enjoy it!

Chapter 1. Getting Started With The Italian Language

Learning a language is a very challenging but fulfilling task. This endeavor tests a person's intellectual capability, speaking skills, and patience in learning something new. If you are thinking of engaging in this challenge, one language that you may consider learning is Italian.

This chapter will give you some of the basic information about the Italian language.

The Italian Language: An Overview

Italian is one of the "Romance languages", along with other popular languages known such as Spanish, Portuguese, and French. As a part of the Romance languages, Italian also gets its roots from Vulgar Latin.

While it is apparent that Italian is mostly spoken in the country of Italy, it is also an official language in some European countries such as Switzerland and Vatican City. Moreover, it is considered as a minority language and is spoken to some extent in other countries. Even France, which mainly speaks French, has some areas where Italian is spoken. According to statistics, almost 15 percent of Europe's population have Italian as their native language, and there are around 85 million speakers around the world. It is also the fourth out of the five Romance languages in terms of its number of speakers (behind French, Portuguese, and Spanish).

Unlike the other Romance languages, Italian retains some of the characteristics present in Latin. This is because Italian contrasts between long and short consonants, and is the closest to Latin when it comes to vocabulary.

Why consider learning Italian?

It was mentioned that Italian only ranks fourth in terms of number of people who speak it. However, this doesn't mean that Italian is not worth learning. In fact, there are many good reasons that are worth considering as to why you might learn Italian.

One reason that Italian is worth learning is that it is highly possible that you already know about some Italian words. Evidence to this is the fact that many of the foods that are served in many parts of the world today are Italian! Some of the most popular foods that have their roots from Italy would be spaghetti, pizza, pasta, espresso, cappuccino, and tiramisu. There are also words that are of Italian origin but are used in English speaking countries when expressing their feelings. Some of the most common expressions are bravo, amore, and ciao.

Another reason that it is worth learning the Italian language is that it shares many cognates with the English language. When you say cognate, this refers to a word in one language which sounds similar and has the same origin as in another language. To better understand what cognates are, let's take a look at the Italian words *aeroporto, medicina,* and *attenzione.* If you read these words in the same way that you read English words, all of these will sound similar to airport, medicine, and attention, respectively. These are the exact meanings of the Italian words previously mentioned. Since many Italian words share this similarity with the English terms that you may be familiar with, it only implies that learning Italian is not as difficult as it seems.

Lastly, the pronunciation of Italian words is not that difficult and seems instinctive. This is especially true if you have knowledge of the English language, where it is a requirement to pronounce each letter in the word. This is unlike other languages, where there are several rules surrounding the pronunciation of words (such as the French liaisons). Further study of Italian pronunciation will be provided in the next chapter.

Now that the basics of the Italian language have been discussed, we will now delve into the important elements that will help you in conversing with other people.

Chapter 2. The Italian Alphabet

To make learning the Italian language easier, it is important that you first learn its basic elements. This chapter will focus on how each letter in the Italian alphabet is pronounced correctly. It will also emphasize on the pronunciation rules of vowels.

Italian alphabet

Words are formed when the letters of the alphabet are combined. Therefore, it is important to first learn about the pronunciation of each letter so that the word can be said correctly.

The table below will be your guide on the letters used in Italian words. The pronunciation of each letter will also be provided for you:

Alphabet	Pronunciation
Aá	ah
Bb	bee
Cc	chee
Dd	dee

Ee	eh
Ff	ehf-feh
Gg	jee
Hh	ahk-kah
Ii	ee
Ll	ehl-leh
Mm	ehm-meh
Nn	ehn-neh
Oo	oh
Pp	Pee
Qq	kooh
Rr	ehr-reh
Ss	ehs-seh
Tt	tee
Uu	ooh
Vv	vooh
Zz	dzeh-tah

As you can see, the Italian alphabet only has 21 letters. The missing letters are j, k, w, x, and y. This explains why no pronunciation is provided for those letters. The pronunciation of each letter is not always used in every word, and these pronunciations are only used when the letters are taken individually (such as when you need to spell out something).

In-depth discussion on the pronunciation of vowels

While it was mentioned that the pronunciation of Italian words are the same as how they are pronounced in English, there are some differences when it comes to the pronunciation of vowels in Italian words. This section will clarify how each vowel is pronounced along with some examples for each.

The vowel "a"

Unlike English, where the pronunciation of this vowel depends on the word (think of the words "salad" and "sale"), this letter only has one pronunciation for the Italians. For them, its pronunciation is similar to the sound of the letter "a" in the word "father" or the sound when you say "ah". This pronunciation is maintained regardless of the word being mentioned.

The following Italian words will depict that this is how this vowel is pronounced, taking note of the underlined area so that the pronunciation of the vowel will be focused:

- *Sale*, which is pronounced as *"s<u>ah</u>-leh"*, is the Italian equivalent for the English word "salt".

- The Italian word *albero,* which means "tree" in English, is properly pronounced as *"<u>ah</u>l-beh-roh"*.

- To pronounce the Italian word *marmellata* (which is "jam" in English) correctly, you must say the word like *"m<u>ah</u>r-mehl-l<u>ah</u>-tah"*.

The vowel "e"

To pronounce this vowel correctly, you need to think about the French word *gourmet* and how the letter "e" in the said word sounds. This pronunciation is very similar to the transcribed sound mentioned in the table above. Here are some Italian words, their meanings, and the application of the pronunciation for the said vowel being underlined:

- The word *bere* is translated in English as "to drink". To pronounce this properly, you simply need to say *"b<u>eh</u>-r<u>eh</u>"*.

- The English word "weight" can be translated in Italian as *peso*. This word is pronounced as *"p<u>eh</u>-zoh"*.

- To pronounce the word *sole*, which means "sun" in English, you need to say it like *"soh-l<u>eh</u>"*.

The vowel "i"

In order to pronounce this vowel properly, you only need to remember how the letters "ee" are said in the English word "see". Take a look at the following Italian words and pronounce them accordingly:

- If you want to say *bimbo* correctly, which is the Italian word for "little boy", say it as if you're reading *"beem-boh"*.

- While the Italian *cinema* has the same meaning as its English counterpart, they differ in the pronunciation. Italians pronounce this word as *"chee-neh-mah"*.

- In order to say *vita* (which means "life") properly, pronounce it as if you're reading *"vee-tah"*.

The vowel "o"

Just like what is listed above, the Italians pronounce the vowel "o" as *"oh"*, similar to when you say "piano". The words below will serve as an example of how the vowel "o" in each word is properly pronounced:

- If you want to include *domain* in your conversation (which means "tomorrow"), you must pronounce it as *"doh-mah-nee"*.

- If you want to say that your food or drink is sweet, you say *dolce* in Italian. This is pronounced as *"dohl-cheh"*.

- If something is little or small, you say *piccolo* in Italian. This word, however, can only be pronounced properly if you say it as *"peek-koh-loh"*.

The vowel "u"

In English, the vowel "u" could have different pronunciations. Just think of the words "utility" and "under" and their differences become obvious. However, Italians pronounce "u" as if you are saying the letters "oo" in the word "zoo". Likewise, this vowel also sounds similar when you say "ooh". The examples below will show the application of this vowel's proper pronunciation:

- The English pronoun "you" is translated in Italian as *tu*. This word can be properly pronounced by saying *"tooh"*.

- When you look at the night sky, you will see the moon, or *luna* in Italian. To say it properly, the word should sound like *"looh-nah"*.

- The English word "fruit" is a cognate of the Italian *frutta*. This word can be pronounced as if you are saying *"frooh-tah"*.

Some peculiarities on vowel pronunciation

While the rules mentioned above are applied in almost every Italian word, there are still cases wherein the intended pronunciation is not used. Here are some examples:

- The Italian word *noi*, which is translated as "we", does not follow the rules regarding the pronunciation of the vowels "o" and "i". If you did try to follow the rules stated above, the word will sound like *"noh-ee"*, which is incorrect. This word must be pronounced as if you're saying *"noy"*, wherein the vowels "oi" must sound like you'll say the English word "oink".

- Another Italian word, *auto* (translated as car), does not follow the rules entirely. While the vowel "o" is pronounced according to the rules, the vowels "a" and "u" are not pronounced as *"ah-ooh"* in compliance with what was mentioned earlier. In this context, *auto* is pronounced as *"ou-toh"*, similar to how you say "ou" in the word "out".

- Lastly, the Italian pronoun *lei* (which is translated as "she") has a different pronunciation as well. The vowels "ei" must sound like "ey" or similar to how you will read "ai" in the English word "aid".

Italian accents and stress

Just like French, the accent is also part of the Italian language. This is because aside from your knowledge of pronunciation rules, the presence of accents helps you in placing the stress on the correct part of the word (unaccented words usually have the stress on its second to the last syllable).

Fortunately, Italians only use two accents – the grave (`) and the acute (´). These accents are usually placed on vowels.

Some Italian words that use accents are the following:

- If you are asking for reasons, you start the sentence with "why", or *perché* in Italian. This is pronounced as *"pehr-keh"*. Since the accent is placed on the last vowel, the stress of the word is given to the syllable where that letter belongs.

- Most people drink coffee, or *caffè*, in the morning. Although the pronunciation, which is *"kahf-feh"*, is unaffected, the position of the accent suggests that the stress must be placed on the last part of the word.

There are many other Italian words whose pronunciations do not follow the general rules for saying the vowels. Make sure to consult the dictionary so that you can add into your vocabulary and understand the proper pronunciation of the word.

Chapter 3. Pronunciation Rules For Consonants

This section will give more emphasis on the pronunciation of Italian consonants, starting from the letters with pronunciations that are instinctive, up to the consonants that have some differences on how they should sound.

The Italian consonants

Just like the vowels, the following consonants have a single pronunciation and do not change regardless of the word where it is used:

- The letter Bb sounds as *"bee"*, just like in the Italian word *bene* which means "well". This word is pronounced as *"beh-neh"* (combining the sounds of b and a).

- Dd is pronounced as *"dee"*. This can be seen in the pronunciation of the Italian word *dare*, or translated as "to give" in English. This word must sound as if you are saying *"dah-reh"*.

- The letter Ff must sound like *"ehf"*. Just take a look at the Italian word *fare* (which is translated as "to make"), which is pronounced as *"fah-reh"*.

- The letter Ll should sound like you are saying *"ehl"*. This pronunciation can be applied in the Italian word *ladro* (which means "thief" in English), which must be said as *"lah-droh"*.

- Letter Mm commonly sounds as *"ehm"*. This can be heard in the Italian word *madre* (which means "mother" in English), which is pronounced as *"mah-dreh"*.

- Nn's pronunciation is instinctive, which is *"ehn"*. Just remember how you'll say the cognate *"no"* in English and you can pronounce any Italian word that has this consonant.

- The letter Pp is pronounced as *"pee"*. Just like in the Italian word *padre* (translated as "father" in English), this is pronounced as *"pah-dreh"*.

- Letter Tt is pronounced as *"tee"*. This can be applied in the Italian word *treno* (translated as "train"), wherein it can be pronounced as *"treh-noh")*. If ever the word features a double "T", just like how the word *spaghetti* is, the letter must be exaggerated or pronounced again. For this word, the pronunciation must be *"spah-geht-tee"*, similar to how you'll say the name Betty.

- Vv is simply pronounced as *"vee"*, just as how you will say the Italian word *vino* (which stands for "wine" in English). This word is properly pronounced simply by saying it like *"vee-noh"*.

Consonants not in Italian vocabulary

As mentioned in the previous section, the letters j, k, w, x, and y are not used in Italian words, which is why no pronunciation is assigned to them. But because some foreign words (primarily English) are currently used in some conversations, the Italians simply use the pronunciation of the word where the letter is found. Only few words are being adapted so that they will have an Italian translation. Some examples include *xenofobia* and *xilofono,* which came from the English words xenophobia and xylophone, respectively.

Discussing the pronunciation of other consonants

As you can observe, the pronunciation of other consonants has not yet been mentioned. This is because of the fact that the way of pronouncing them changes depending on certain conditions. This section will enumerate how these consonants can be pronounced properly for each condition.

Pronouncing the letter "C"

The Italians pronounce this letter in two different ways, and the pronunciation depends on the letter that comes after "C".

If letter "C" is followed by the vowels a, o, and u, or is followed by any other consonant, its pronunciation is the same with how you'll say the English word "cat" (adapting

14

the sound of the English letter "K"). This can also be called as the "Hard C" pronunciation.

Some of the words that adapt this pronunciation are the following:

- If you would want to say "house" in Italian, you need to say *casa*. Pronounced as *"kah-sah"*, you can see that the letter C adapts the sound of letter K.

- One of the most important parts of the body is the heart, or *cuore* in Italian. This can be pronounced as *"kwoh-reh"*.

- If you would like to refer to the feeling of guilt, you say the Italian word *colpa*, which is pronounced as *"kohl-pah"*.

Although it is implied that the hard C pronunciation will not be adapted if the letter "C" is followed by the vowels e and i, it is still possible for words that fit this category to have C pronounced as K if the letter H is found between C and any vowel. Take a look at the following words:

- If you need to ask something that starts with the word "what", it is said in Italian as *che*, which is properly pronounced by saying it as *"keh"* (adapting the sound of K).

- If today is Sunday, you need to go to church, or *chiesa* in Italian. This word is properly pronounced by saying it as *"kyeh-zah"*.

- In order to unlock a door, you need a *chiave* (or key in English). To pronounce it properly, the word must sound like you're saying *"kyah-veh"*.

On the other hand, if letter C is followed by the vowels e and i, the letter adapts the so-called "soft C" pronunciation. For this type of pronunciation, the letter C must sound like you are saying it with an h, or must sound like "ch" (like how you say these letters in the English word "church").

The following are just some of the Italian words that adapt this kind of pronunciation:

- They say that sharing food (translated as *cibo*), particularly dinner (translated as *cena*), can help improve the relationship of family members. Those Italian words, since they fall on the category stated above, must be pronounced as *"chee-boh"* and *"cheh-nah"*, respectively.

- The English adverb "certainly" is said to express agreement on something, and this can be translated in Italian as *certo*. But if you want to include this word in your sentence, you need to say it properly, which can be done by saying it as *"chehr-toh"*.

The "soft C" pronunciation is also applied if C is followed by the other vowels, as long as the letter "I" is found between C and the vowels a, o, and u. The letter "I", though, is only written for the purpose of producing the "ch" sound and must not be pronounced.

Take a look at the examples below to better understand this concept:

- The "almost universal" Italian greeting *ciao* (which means "hello" or "goodbye") is properly pronounced as *"chou"*.

- If you're finding it hard to make your baby stop crying, you need to use a pacifier or *ciuccio* for the Italians. To properly pronounce it, the word must sound like you're saying *"chooh-choh"*.

- Almost everybody loves sweets, especially chocolates (or *cioccolata* for the Italians). Sounding like how the Americans say "chocolate" in English, its Italian equivalent is pronounced as *"chok-koh-lah-tah"*.

- If you have been to the coffee shop, you may have ordered the *cappuccino*, or coffee that was made with milk. For this word, take a look at the pronunciation of *–cino,* as it made use of the "soft C" pronunciation.

While the rules above may seem a bit complex for beginners, these are mostly instinctive due to the similarity of the two languages. However, if you are in doubt as to the pronunciation of an Italian word that you've never seen before and has a letter C in it, the rules for pronunciation can be summarized into two:

- If the letter C is followed by the vowels I and E, use the soft C pronunciation ("ch").

- If the letter C is followed by the vowels A, O, and U, and any other consonant, use the hard C pronunciation ("K" sound).

Pronouncing the letter "G"

If you are already familiar with the rules in pronouncing the letter "C", doing the same for Italian words that have the letter "G" will be a breeze. This is because just like the former, the letter G also has a hard and soft pronunciation.

The Hard G pronunciation is applied if the letter that comes after G are the vowels a, o, and u. This same pronunciation is also applied if it is followed by other consonants. Just remember how the English word "good" is pronounced, as this is the exact sound that must be made for the hard G pronunciation.

The points below will give you an idea as to how this pronunciation is applied in Italian words that have this letter:

- An integral part of the body that aids in movement is the leg, or translated as *gamba*. This word must be pronounced as *"gahm-bah"* if you want it to sound correct.

- Tires are made of rubber, or *gomma* in Italian. To say this word correctly, it must sound like *"gohm-mah"*.

- If you are a peace-loving person, then you are not the type to wage war, or *guerra* in Italian. This can be pronounced correctly by saying it as *"gweh-rah"*.

It is also possible to get the sound of a hard G pronunciation if it comes before the vowels e and i, provided that the letter h is between G and the vowels e or i.

The following words will demonstrate the application of this rule:

- The popular Italian food (and word) *spaghetti* makes use of the hard g pronunciation, as it can be pronounced as *"spah-geht-tee"*.

- Serving a cold drink is possible with the help of ice, or *ghiaccio* for the Italians. To sound like a native speaker, it must be pronounced as *"gyahch-choh"*.

- When Christmas season is in the air, many homes place wreaths, or *ghirlanda*. This word must sound like you're saying *"geer-lahn-dah"*.

Likewise, there is also a "soft" pronunciation for letter G. Similar to the rules for letter C, the soft G pronunciation is applied if the letter that comes after G is either the vowel e or i. The sound that must be made is similar to the English letter J, or the first sound that you make when you say the English word "job".

Here are some examples which apply this pronunciation rule:

- If a person is kind, they can be referred in Italian as *gentile*. To say this properly, the word must be pronounced as *"jehn-tee-leh"*.

- If you are referring to the English word "day", it is translated as *giorno* in Italian. Applying the soft G pronunciation, this word must sound like you're saying *"johr-noh"*.

- If you want to express jealousy in Italian, you simply say *gelosia*. This is properly pronounced by saying it as *"jeh-loh-zee-ah")*.

It is also possible to produce the "j" sound if the letter G is followed by the other vowels as long as the letter "I" is found between them. Just like the rule in the soft C pronunciation, the letter "I" is only placed to indicate the proper pronunciation of the word. Aside from the previously mentioned Italian word *giorno*, other Italian words that comply with this rule are the following:

- If you are on a court hearing, your case is looked at by the judge, or *giudice* in Italian. This word is properly pronounced by saying it as *"jooh-dee-cheh"*.

- If you want something fun, play a *gioco*, which is the Italian word for game. This can be pronounced correctly if you say it as *"joh-koh"*.

- Wearing a jacket, or *giacca,* is a must during the winter. You can say this Italian word correctly if you pronounce it as *"jahk-kah"*.

The principle used in remembering when to apply the hard and soft pronunciation for C is also used for the pronunciation of G.

Pronouncing the letter "H"

This consonant has only one purpose in the Italian language – that is, if it is seen after letter C or G and is followed by the vowels e and i, it requires the speaker to use the hard pronunciation (as seen in the examples above). But even if it does appear on some foreign words such as hobby or hostess, this letter is <u>ALWAYS</u> silent (just like in speaking French).

Pronouncing the letter "Q"

While the sound of this letter is somewhat similar to the letter K, it is mostly seen connected to the letter U and is always followed by another vowel. This only means that you will always find "qu" (pronounced as "kw") for Italian words that start with this letter.

Some Italian words that start with Q, along with their pronunciations, are found below:

- If you want to remember a certain event or place, you usually take a picture (or *quadro*). To say it properly, your pronunciation must be the same as *"kwah-droh"*.

- If you want to buy something, you pay using money, or *quattrini*. This word can be pronounced correctly if you say it as *"kwaht-tree-neeh"*.

- One important event in the Catholic's liturgical year is Lent, or *quaresima*. This can be pronounced by saying it as *"kwah-reh-see-mah"*.

Pronouncing the letter "R"

Italians have a different way of pronouncing the letter R. If you are used to the English language, this letter is pronounced with your tongue curved towards your uvula. For Italians, pronouncing the same letter is done by vibrating your tongue while it is placed behind the front teeth. Obviously, the movement of the tongue creates a vibrating sound for the letter, and is the cue that you can look at if you want to be able to pronounce it correctly.

Here are some of the words that could help you to practice your pronunciation of the said letter:

- The cognate word *radio* has a different pronunciation for the Italians. If English speakers pronounce the word as *"ray-dee-ow"*, Italians pronounce it as *"rah-dee-oh"*.

- Saying *per favore*, or please, can help convey humility and develop your tongue when saying other Italian words that have the letter R. This word is pronounced as *"pehr fah-voh-reh"*.

- If somebody thanked you for doing something for them, you say "You're welcome". This same expression is translated as *prego* in Italian, and is pronounced as *"preh-goh"*.

Pronouncing the letter "S"

The Italian letter S has a similar pronunciation with what is used in the English language, as its sound is close to what is produced when you say the word "so" or "snake".

Some of the words that follow this rule would be the Italian words *pasta* and *solo*, which are already adapted in the English vocabulary. These words are pronounced as *"pahs-tah"* and *"soh-loh"*, respectively. In this example, you can see that both words adapt the "S" sound.

However, there are some cases wherein the Italian letter S takes the sound of the English letter Z, as if you're saying the word "zero". One rule that is applied in many cases as regards to when the letter S must adapt the sound of letter Z is if the S is found in between two vowels. Some of the words that follow this pronunciation rule are *chiesa* (wherein S is found between the vowels e and a) and *gelosia* (S is in the middle of the vowels o and i), both of which were mentioned earlier. Although the focus of these words was different earlier, both of them adapted the sound of letter Z when pronouncing the letter S. This rule though, has some exceptions.

Pronouncing the letter "Z"

Just like the letter S, pronouncing the Italian Z is similar to its English counterpart. The only difference between the two languages is that the Italians usually add a "d" at the beginning, making it sound like "dz". If you are to pronounce the word *zero* in Italian, it sounds like *"dzehr-oh"*.

If ever you find Italian words that have a double Z, such as *tazza* (mug or cup in English), the pronunciation is sharper and sounds more like *"t-ts"*. In this example, *tazza* is pronounced as *"that-tsah"*.

Another applicable rule for pronouncing letter Z is if it's followed by the letter I, it also adapts the "ts" sound. This can be seen in the Italian word *nazione* (translated as "nation" in English), which is pronounced as *"nah-tsyoh-neh"*.

Encountering words with double consonants

If you are looking at Italian dictionaries, you might observe that some words have double consonants. In order to say these words properly, you need to make sure that each consonant is pronounced. This can be difficult for those who are used to the English language, as the part where the double consonant is seen usually gets a single sound even if two of the same letters are written. But as you practice, doing this will be easier.

One guideline that you can follow when it comes to pronouncing words with double consonants is to say it as part of the previous syllable, and also emphasize it as part of the next. Emphasizing double consonants is important in Italian, as there are words whose meanings will be changed if no emphasis was provided in the pronunciation.

To better understand this, take a look at the Italian words *nono* and *nonno*. If you pronounce these words using English, you will most likely end up sounding the same no matter which word you say. However, for Italians, it is necessary that you make the second word sound like it has a doubled letter N. This is because you may convey the meaning of "grandfather" (for *nonno*) even if what you want to say is "ninth" (*nono*). To pronounce *nono* and *nonno* correctly, you must say the first as *"noh-noh"* and the second as *"nohn-noh"*. For the second pronunciation, the sound of the "doubled N" is obvious, as the emphasis is present on both the first and next syllable.

To better apply your knowledge in pronouncing double consonants, take a look at the following Italian words:

- If you want to compliment another person's physical appearance, one word that is often used is beautiful, or *bello*. To say this word properly, it must be said as *"behl-loh"*.

- The beach, or *spiaggia*, is a good place to go for the summer. But in order to invite your friends to the right place, this word must be pronounced as *"spyahj-jah"*.

- Wearing a hat, or *cappello*, is done to shield you from the heat of the sun. However, make sure that you pronounce it as *"kahp-peh-loh"*! Because if not, you might end up conveying the similar sounding Italian word *capello* (which means "hair", and is pronounced as *"kah-pehl-loh"*.

Pronunciation of Italian consonant clusters

Although the pronunciation of Italian letters are not very different from English, there are certain consonant clusters in the language whose sounds are different than if they were pronounced using the rules previously mentioned.

These clusters are as follows:

- gl – for Italian words that contain this cluster, the pronunciation is changed to "ly", similar to the sound created when you say "ll" in the English word "million". Words that make use of this cluster are *gli* (equivalent to the English determiner "the") and *famiglia* (cognate for the English word "family"). Applying this pronunciation rule, these words must sound like *"lyee"* and *"fah-mee-lyah"*, respectively. The letter "g" in the cluster is treated as a silent letter.

- gn – the pronunciation for this consonant cluster is similar to gl. The only difference is the sound that it makes, which is similar to "ny". You can also think of its sound when you say the letter "ñ" in Spanish word *señorito* (mister). An Italian word that makes use of this consonant cluster is *gnocchi* (pronounced as *"nyohk-kee"*), an Italian dish.

- sc – this consonant cluster follows the soft and hard c pronunciation guidelines. If this cluster is followed by a, o, u, or h, its pronunciation is similar to the English word "scooter". Some words that follow this rule are *sconto* (translated as "discount", and is pronounced as *"skohn-toh"*), *scuola* ("school" in English, and is pronounced as *"skwoh-lah"*), and *scala* (or "scale" in English, said as *"skah-lah"*). On the other hand, if the cluster is followed by e or i, it adapts the soft pronunciation, or how "sh" is said in the word "shampoo". Examples for this rule are *scesa* ("descent" in English, pronounced as *"sheh-sah"*) and *scimmia* (translated as "monkey", and pronounced as *"sheem-mee-ah"*).

Mastering the basics in letter pronunciation will allow you to speak correctly so that you can convey what you really want to say. This sets you up for conversing using Italian.

Chapter 4. Date, Time, And Numbers In Italian

Now that you know the basics of letter pronunciation, you can now start engaging in conversations. And some of the most common topics in many conversations include dates, numbers, and time. This section will teach you about the phrases and systems used in order to count, and tell the dates and time using Italian.

Days of the week and the months of the year

In the Italian language, the first letter of the days of the week and the months of the year are not written in capital letters.

The table below will show you the Italian equivalent of each day:

Day	Italian equivalent	Pronunciation
Monday	lunedi	Loo-neh-dee
Tuesday	martedi	Mahr-the-dee
Wednesday	mercoledi	Mehk-koh-leh-dee
Thursday	giovedi	Zhoh-veh-dee

Friday	venerdi	Veh-nehr-dee
Saturday	sabato	Sah-bah-toh
Sunday	domenica	Doh-meh-nee-kah

The table below will serve as a guide on the months of the year:

Month	Italian equivalent	Pronunciation
January	gennaio	Jehn-nah-yoh
February	febbraio	Fehb-brah-yoh
March	marzo	Mahr-tsoh
April	aprile	Ah-pree-leh
May	maggio	Mahj-joh
June	giugno	Joo-nyoh
July	luglio	Loo-lyoh
August	agosto	Ah-gohs-toh
September	settembre	Seht-tehm-breh
October	ottobre	Oht-toh-breh

| November | novembre | Noh-vehm-breh |
| December | dicembre | Dee-chehm-breh |

When writing the date, write the day first, followed by the month, and lastly the year. Following this format is crucial, especially if you will be writing the month as a number. For example, if you would want to write May 8, 2015, it must be written as 08/05/2015. If you write it as the usual 05/08/2015 format, your companion might assume that the date you're referring to is August 5, 2015.

Here are other phrases that will help you in conversations regarding dates:

- If you want to ask "What day is today?" or "What is the date?" in Italian, you say it as *"Che giorno è oggi?"*

- If you are being asked of the day and your answer is Wednesday, you must say it as *"Oggi è mercoledi"*.

- An informal way to ask another person about their birthday in Italian is *"Quando è il tuo compleanno?"*

- If somebody asks you about the date and you would want to answer that it's May 8, your answer must be *"Il otto maggio"*. In this answer, it can be seen that the syntax still follows the format that the Italians use when they give the date. For the translation of numbers in Italian, see next section.

Italian style counting

Another area that is often included in conversations revolves around numbers. This is especially true if you are in a marketplace and you're paying for the item that you want to buy. With enough knowledge of counting, transactions will be significantly easier for both parties.

Fortunately, there is a distinguishable pattern that is similar to what is applied in English. This makes it easy for anyone to memorize and remember how each number must be said.

In the Italian system, numbers 0 to 16 have unique names, making it very similar to English. After this, you simply need to add the succeeding numbers to the tens place and make it as a single word. For example, if you want to translate the number 18 in Italian, you simply need to combine the Italian equivalent for the numbers 10 and 8.

The table below shows the Italian equivalent for numbers 0 to 19:

Number	Italian Equivalent
0	zero
1	uno

2	due
3	tre
4	quattro
5	cinque
6	Sei
7	sette
8	otto
9	nove
10	dieci
11	undici
12	dodici
13	tredici
14	quattordici
15	quindici
16	sedici
17	diciasette
18	diciotto
19	diciannove

You also need to remember the names for the other tens place. Once you do, you simply need to add the Italian equivalents for numbers 1 to 9. But aside from this guideline, you also need to remember that when combining the numbers 1 and 8 to the tens place, you need to drop the final letter and replace it with the first letter of those numbers. For example, if you need to say 21, you don't say it as *ventiuno*. Rather, you replace "i" with the first letter of *uno*. Therefore, the number 21 is translated as *ventuno*.

The table below will serve as your guide for counting numbers 20 to 99:

Number	Italian Equivalent
20	venti
21	ventuno
22	ventidue
23	ventitrè
28	ventotto
30	trenta
31	trentuno

40	quaranta
41	quarantuno
50	cinquanta
60	sessanta
70	settanta
80	ottanta
90	novanta

Another guideline to remember is that when you add *tre* in counting, its vowel takes an accent, making it as *trè*.

The same pattern applied in tens is also applied in larger numbers. The table below will guide you in counting or saying larger numbers:

Number	Italian Equivalent
100	cento
101	centuno
102	centodue
120	centoventi
150	centocinquanta

200	duecento
1000	mille
2000	duemila

When saying large numbers, the order of saying it is similar to how it is said in English. For example, if you want to say 1950 in Italian, you will say *millenovecentocinquanta* (which is literally translated as one thousand nine hundred fifty).

Here are other phrases that may be used which have something to do with numbers:

- When asking for the price, it is said as "How much is it?" in English. To say this same phrase in Italian, you must say *"Quanto viene?"*

- If you want to ask the question "How old are you?" in Italian, remember the phrase *"Quanti anni hai?"*

- If you are a seller and you want to say that the item costs 5 euros and 60 cents, you say it as *"cinque euro sessanta"*.

- If you were the one asked about your age and your answer is "I am 26 years old", your response must be *"Ho ventisei anni"*.

Telling time in Italian

Once you know the numbers, it is easier to tell the time when somebody asks you or vice versa. You simply need to remember some guidelines:

- Italians use the 24 hour clock, whether in writing or conversation. This simply means that you'll be adding 12 to the current time if it's after noon. For example, if you are referring to 10 in the evening, this is equivalent to 22. Therefore, you will be saying the Italian equivalent of that number (which is *ventidue*).

- Italians write time using commas, not colons, which is different from what can be seen in English documents. This means that rather than writing 1:30 PM, Italians write it as 1,30 PM or even 13,30.

- When Italians tell time, they start by saying the hour followed by the minute. For example, if the time is 3:23 PM, they say it as *le quindici e ventitrè*. However, this is different when the time is past half hour. Once this happens, Italians refer to the next hour and the number of minutes left before the hour comes. For example, if the time is 3:45 PM, you will be saying *le sedici meno un quarto* (which is translated as "a quarter to 4 PM).

The table below will serve as your guide in telling the time using the Italian language:

English statement	Italian equivalent
It's midnight	È mezzanotte
It's noon	È mezzogiorno
It's 12:30 in the afternoon	È mezzogiorno e mezzo
It's 1:00 AM	È l'una
It's 1:10 AM	È l'una e dieci
It's 1:15 AM	È l'una e un quarto
It's 1:50 AM	*Sono le due meno dieci* (literally translated as "It's 10 minutes before 2 AM)

Here are other phrases that must be remembered if you are referring to time at a general sense:

English statement	Italian equivalent
Today	oggi
Tomorrow	domain
Yesterday	ieri
Midnight	mezzanotte
Noon	mezzogiorno

Day	giorno
In the middle of the night (can also refer until 5 in the morning)	di note
In the evening	di sera
In the afternoon	del pomeriggio
In the morning	di mattina
Day after tomorrow	dopodomani

By knowing the rules and guidelines that revolve around telling dates, time, and numbers, you can engage in more conversations and be able to understand when these terms are involved.

Chapter 5. Italian Grammar Rules For Nouns

Once you have knowledge about the pronunciation rules and have enriched your vocabulary, you can better engage in conversations. This is why it is necessary to learn about the grammar rules of the Italian language.

This chapter will focus on the rules of the language when it comes to the use of nouns.

Masculine and feminine nouns

Italians noun have a gender, and they can either be masculine or feminine. While the gender of the noun can be distinguished by looking at the article (which is not the focus of this chapter), it is possible to learn of the gender by looking at the noun itself.

Here are some guidelines that you can follow in determining the gender of the noun:

- If the noun is ending with the letter –o, it is usually masculine. For example, the Italian words *l'uomo* and *il fratello* are translated as "man" and "brother", respectively, in English. This rule applies to all nouns, even to those which are nonliving. Some Italian words that show this rule are *il treno* (translated as "train") and *il pomeriggio*. Because these words comply with this rule, they are ascribed with the masculine gender.

- If the noun is ending with the letter –a, it is usually ascribed as feminine. This can be seen on words such as *la donna* and *la sorella*, which are translated as "woman" and "sister", respectively, in English. This is also applied on nonliving nouns such as *la bicicletta* and *la sera,* which means "bicycle" and "evening", respectively.

- If a noun is ending with the letter –e, its gender can either be masculine or feminine. Unfortunately, it can be difficult to determine the gender of the noun if it ends with this letter. For example, the words *ristorante* and *colome* (which means "restaurant" and "surname", respectively) are ascribed with the masculine gender while the words *notte* (night) and *chiave* (key) are ascribed as feminine. The only way to do so is if the word already has a defined gender, such as *padre* (father) and *madre* (mother), if the gender can be identified by the person being referred by the noun (for example, the word *cantate* or singer can have a specific gender depending on the person), or if you memorize the ascribed gender of the words that ends with -e.

In order to identify the gender of some nouns that are ending in the letter –e, look at the last part of the word. If the noun is ending in –zione or –zione, its gender is feminine. For example, the Italian words *television* (television), *stazione* (station), and *produzione* (production) are treated as feminine nouns.

- An Italian noun that is referring to a person and ends with the letter –a will have a gender that corresponds to the person that is associated with the word. Let's take a look at the Italian words *pianista* (pianist), and *collega* (colleague). If the rule mentioned above is followed, it is easily concluded that the gender ascribed to these words are feminine. However, the words themselves will only have a distinguishable gender depending on the person that is associated with it. Therefore, if the phrases are *il pianista* and *il collega* (wherein *il* is similar to the English pronoun "he"), these words will have a masculine gender. Likewise, if the phrases are *la pianista* and *la collega* (wherein *la* can be translated as the English pronoun "she"), the nouns will be ascribed as feminine.

- Some nouns, even if they end with –a, have a masculine gender. This also applies to its counterpart, as there are nouns which end with –o but have a feminine gender. For example, the nouns *cinema* and *problema* (problem) are ascribed as masculine and are mostly written as *il cinema* and *il problema*. Likewise, the words such as *foto* (photo)

41

and *mano* (hand) have a feminine gender, and are mostly written as *la foto* and *la mano*.

- Most of the nouns that end in –i are ascribed as feminine. Some examples include the Italian words *crisi* (crisis), *l'analisi* (analysis), and *l'ipotesi* (hypothesis). However, there are words which fall in this category but are ascribed as masculine. The words *lo sci* (ski) and *l'alibi* (alibi) are some of those exempted to this rule.

- If a foreign noun is to be used, the gender that is ascribed to it follows the gender that is attached to its Italian equivalent. Take a look at the English word "e-mail message", which is translated as *la mail*. In order to determine its gender, "mail" is translated in Italian, which is equivalent to *posta*. Since it ends with –a, it acquires the feminine gender.

- If a foreign noun does not have an Italian equivalent, it is generally ascribed as masculine. However, if the noun is referring to a female person, this is the only time that the gender ascribed to it is changed.

- The names of all languages are always ascribed as masculine.

- If the name of a country is ending with –a, it is regarded as feminine. However, if it ends with any other letter, it is ascribed as masculine. For example, the Italian equivalent for the countries *Francia* (France) and *Spagna* (Spain) are regarded as feminine, while the country *Belgio* (Belgium) has a masculine gender.

- All days of the week are regarded as masculine, except for *domenica*, which is ascribed as feminine.

Singular and plural nouns

Quantity is also an important component surrounding nouns, as they can either be singular or plural. This section will enumerate the guidelines that are used if you want to turn singular nouns into their plural forms.

- If you want to pluralize masculine nouns that are ending in −o and any noun that is ending in −e, you simply need to replace the last letter with −i.

To better understand the application of this rule, take a look at the following examples:

English noun	Italian singular	Italian plural
Name	il nome	i nomi
Night	la notte	le notti
Pension	la pensione	le pensioni
Relative	il/la parente	i/le parenti

43

Station	la stazione	le stazioni
Train	il treno	i treni

In this table, it can be seen that once the last letter of each Italian singular noun is changed into –i, it is automatically regarded as plural. If ever you encounter words whose singular form ends with an –ie, such as *la moglie* (or wife), it can be changed to its plural form by simply removing the last letter so that its ending is –i. In this particular example, the plural form of the said word would be *le mogli*.

- If the noun is ending with –io, you only need to remove the last letter so that the word will have an –i ending and will make it plural. For example, if you want to pluralize the Italian word *il bacio* (translated as "kiss"), you only need to remove –o and make it as *i baci* (kisses) to make it plural. This also follows for the words *l'inizio* (beginning in English) and *il desiderio* (or wish), which can be pluralized by writing or pronouncing them as *gli inizi* (beginnings) and *i desideri* (wishes). However, if the –io ending of the word has a stressed –i, it can be pluralized by simply changing –o into –i as well. Some of the words that follow this rule are *lo zio* (which means "uncle") and *il mormorio* (murmur). Because of the stress, these nouns can be turned into a plural by making them into *gli zii* (uncles) and *i mormorii* (murmurs), respectively.

- If the noun is ending with an −a and is ascribed as feminine, it can be turned into its plural form by changing −a into −e. Let's take a look at the previously mentioned Italian words *la sorella* and *la sera*. To turn them into their plural form, simply change the last letter to −e, writing or saying these words as *le sorelle* (sisters) and *le sere* (evenings), respectively.

- If the noun ending in −a is a masculine, it can be changed to its plural form by changing its last letter to −i. Take a look at the Italian nouns *il problema* (problem) and *il sistema* (system). Applying the rule stated above, the plural form of these nouns in Italian will be *i problem* (problems) and *i sistemi* (systems), respectively.

- If a noun ending in −a is referring to a person, changing it to plural form depends on the gender associated with it. If the noun pertains to a male, it takes the masculine gender and can be pluralized by changing the ending to −i. On the other hand, if the noun pertains to a female, the feminine gender is ascribed and can be changed in its plural form by replacing its last letter with −e. Take a look at the previously mentioned Italian word *pianista*. If the pronoun before the word is *il* (equivalent to "he"), it takes the masculine gender and can be pluralized by writing it as *i pianisti* (translated as "male pianists). On the other hand, if it is preceded by the Italian pronoun *la* (equivalent to "she"), it takes the feminine gender and will be changed into plural by writing it as *le pianiste* (translated as "female pianists").

- If a noun in its singular form is already ending with −i, no change is made for it to become plural. Take a look at the previously mentioned terms *l'analisi* and *la crisi*. To change these nouns into their plural forms, only the articles will be changed but the noun itself is not. In this example, these nouns will be in their plural form if they are written as *le analisi* (analyses) and *le crisi* (crises).

- If you encounter foreign nouns or Italian nouns which have a stress in their last vowel, the word remains unchanged even in its plural form. Similar to the previous guideline, the plural form of the noun is only distinguished by looking at the article that precedes it. For foreign nouns, take a look at the words *il bar* (referring to an establishment bar) and *lo sport*. As foreign words adapted in the Italian language, they can be turned into plural if they are written as *i bar* and *gli sport*. It can be noticed that only the word preceding the noun is changed, but this is an indicator that the noun is pluralized. For Italian nouns which are stressed, take a look at the words *la città* (city) and *la virtù* (virtue). These nouns can be pluralized by changing them into *le città* (cities) and *le virtù* (virtues), respectively. Again, it can be seen that only the article before the noun is changed to make it plural.

- There are some nouns that are initially masculine in their singular forms but became feminine when changed to plural. To better understand this concept, take a look at the Italian noun *il dito* (translated as "finger" in English). Since it ends with −o, the noun is ascribed with the masculine gender. However, if this noun is changed into its plural form, it becomes *le dita* (or "fingers"). Since the plural form is ending with the letter −a, it is ascribed with the feminine gender.

- If the noun is ending with −ca or −ga and must be changed to its plural form, the last letter must be changed with −e and should have an additional −h in between (making the ending as −che or −ghe). This is done so that the noun will retain the hard C and G pronunciation of the word. To understand this concept, take a look at the Italian nouns *l'amica* (translated as "female friend"), *la riga* (translated as either "lines" or "ruler" as the measuring tool), and *la tasca* ("pocket" in English). Going back to the previous rule on pronunciation, these words have a hard pronunciation because the letters C and

47

G are followed by the letter a. Since these words are ending with −a, they are ascribed as feminine and therefore can be turned to plural by changing the said letter with −e. However, doing this so will change the word's pronunciation into soft C and G. This can be prevented by simply adding −h in between the letters. For these words, they can be turned into plural by writing them as *le amiche* (friends), *le righe* (lines or rulers), and *le tasche* (pockets).

- The previous guideline can also be followed if the singular form of the Italian noun is ending with −co or −go. This time, the −o will be changed with −i and −h will be added in the middle, making it become −chi or −ghi. This is also made to retain the hard C and G pronunciation. Take a look at the Italian nouns *il bosco* (wood) and *il parco* (park). Applying this rule, these nouns can be changed into their plural forms by writing them as *i boschi* (woods) and *i parchi* (parks), respectively. However, not all Italian words that end in −co or −go follow this rule, as some nouns can be changed into plural by simply changing the last letter into −i and not inserting −h in between. Take a look at the words *il biologo* (biologist) and *il medico* (doctor). These words can be turned into their plural forms without the −h, making them as *i biologi* (doctors) and *i medici* (doctors), respectively.

- If the noun is ending in –cia or –gia, the last letter will be changed to –e and will retain –i if that letter is stressed or if a vowel comes before the letters –c and –g. Take a look at the Italian verb *la farmacia* (pharmacy). Since –i is stressed due to it being included in the "second to the last syllable is stressed" rule, it will follow the guideline that was stated and will be *le farmacie* (pharmacies) in its plural form. However, if the letter that comes before the –cia or –gia is a consonant, the –i is lost while – a is changed to –e in its plural form. As an example to this rule, take a look at the Italian noun *l'arancia* (orange). Since the letter N (which is a consonant) is written before –cia, this rule will take effect and the plural form of this noun will become *le arance* (oranges).

Memorizing these rules on nouns will help you to converse or write sentences correctly. While it may seem plenty, you can exercise your knowledge of these rules by checking the Italian dictionary and try to see if you can recognize the gender of the noun and convert them into plural or singular.

Chapter 6. An Introduction To Italian Articles

Another important part of Italian grammar is the use of articles. In the previous chapter, some of the articles were already mentioned. But how will you know which article must be used? Which article is correct or incorrect?

This chapter will focus on the Italian articles. It will also enumerate the guidelines that must be considered as to when an article must be used.

Definite article

In English, their definite article is "the". In the Italian language, although their definite article is similar to what is used in English, it comes in different forms. The form of the definite article is an indicator of the gender (whether masculine or feminine) and the quantity (whether singular or plural) of the noun that follows it. The definite article also depends on the first letter of the word that is following it.

The table below will show the different forms of the English article "the" in Italian:

	Singular	Plural
Masculine	il	i

	lo	gli
	l'	gli
Feminine	la	le
	l'	le

The guidelines for the use of these article forms are as follows:

- If the word is ascribed as feminine, it uses the feminine forms. Depending on its quantity, the appropriate form of the article must be used. If the word is singular and starts with a consonant, *la* will be used. For example, the word *stanza* (room) must be written as *la stanza* because it starts with S. On the other hand, if the word is starting with a vowel or with an h, l' will be used and have it contracted with the word. For example, the words *esperienza* (experience) and *hostess* (stewardess) must be preceded by the definite article *l,* making them into *l'esperienza* and *l'hostess,* respectively. If the word is changed to its plural form, simply change the article into *le*, regardless of the form that was earlier used. For the words mentioned above, if they are turned plural, they are now written as *le stanze, le esperienza,* and *le hostess*, respectively.

- The articles under the masculine row are used if the word where the article is connected to is ascribed as masculine. Just like the previous guideline, the article *l'* is used for words that start with a vowel or h. For example, the word *hotel* can be attached with *l'*, making it as *l'hotel*. For the article *lo,* it is used if the word is starting with the letters x, y, z, ps, gn, s followed by a consonant, and i followed by a vowel. For example, the words *spettacolo* (show), *zio* (uncle), and *psicologo* (psychologist) must be preceded by *lo* and will make them as *lo spettacolo, lo zio,* and *lo psicologo.* For singular words that do not fit any of the guidelines mentioned, *il* is used as the article. For the plural forms of the word, *i* is used to replace the singular article *il,* while *gli* is used to replace both *l'* and *lo.*

- If the last letter of the noun is −e or −a, it can refer to either of the genders. Therefore, one must be careful as to which article must be placed. For example, the singular noun *cantante* (singer) can refer to either a male or a female singer. If you use the article *il,* this conveys the message that you are referring to a male singer. Likewise, using *la* before the word implies that the singer is a female.

Indefinite articles

The Italians also have their own indefinite article, similar to "a" and/or "an" used in English. The use of Italian indefinite articles depend on the gender and the first letter (or sound) made by the word that follows it, and these articles do not have a plural form. These indefinite articles are the following:

Gender	Indefinite article
Masculine	un uno
Feminine	un' una

The guidelines as to the use of these articles are as follows:

- The indefinite articles *un'* and *una* are used if the word before it is ascribed as feminine. *Un'* is placed before the word if it starts with the letter h or a vowel. For example, if you want to translate "a hostess" or "a car" in Italian, it is written as *un' hostess* and *un' auto*, respectively. On the other hand, *una* is used if the next word starts with a consonant. For example, the phrase "a room" can be translated in Italian as *una stanza*.

- The indefinite articles *uno* and *un* are used if the word after it is ascribed as masculine. *Uno* is used if the next word starts with z, ps, gn, s followed by a consonant, or if the word is masculine and starts with letter i followed by a vowel, x, and y. For example, if you're referring to "a psychologist", its translation will be *uno psicologo*. If the next word does not follow the category for using *uno*, *un* is used instead. For example, the phrase "an article" is *un articolo* in Italian.

- One must also be careful when using indefinite articles on words which are ending in −e and −a, as the message that may be conveyed can be different if the incorrect article is used. For example, if you are referring to a male singer, make sure that you write or say *un cantante*. This is because writing *una cantante* gives the message that the singer is female (because the feminine indefinite article was used).

By becoming familiar with the correct article to use in your phrase or sentence, you will be able to convey the correct message to your listener and make conversations clearer.

Chapter 7. Common Italian Phrases

Learning Italian entails that you need to spend some time practicing in order to become proficient with it. However, this doesn't mean that you cannot speak the language without mastering it. You can start by learning important Italian phrases that are used in many conversations. It is also one way of getting immersed with the language and further master it.

This chapter will enumerate common Italian phrases that are worth memorizing.

Greetings and introductions

- *Buongiorno!* is a greeting that stands for Hello and/or Good morning! To pronounce it properly, say it like *bwohn-johr-noh*

- If you are speaking to somebody that you know, one informal greeting that you can say to them is *Ciao!* (*chou*) This greeting stands for either "Hello!" or "Good-bye!"

- If you are not sure if an informal greeting sounds rude or not to the other person, it's better to extend a neutral greeting such as *salve* (*sahl-veh*). This greeting also means "Hello!" or "Good-bye!", but is not too formal and not too informal.

- If you are aiming for a formal tone and you want to say "Goodbye", say *arrivederci! (ahr-ree-veh-dehr-chee)*

- If the meeting is in the afternoon, you can start the conversation by saying *buon pomeriggio.* This greeting is translated as "Good afternoon", and is pronounced as *bwohn poh-meh-ree-jhoh.*

- Another way of saying "Good afternoon" in a formal way is *buonasera. (bwoh-nah-seh-rah).* Fortunately, this can also be used to greet somebody with "Good evening".

- A more informal tone of saying "Good evening" is "Good Night". This message can be conveyed by saying *buonanotte (bwoh-nah-noht-teh).*

- The phrase "How are you?" is a common question that is not only asked when meeting with friends. It can also be asked if you are meeting a person for the first time. This question can be asked in a formal manner by saying *Come sta? (koh-meh stah).* But if you are talking to someone you know, the more informal *Come stai? (koh-meh stahy)* will suffice.

- Want to ask for somebody's name? You can do so by saying the phrases *Come si chiama? (koh-meh see kyah-mah*) or *Come ti chiami?* (*koh-meh tee kyah-mee*). The first greeting is considered as a formal way of asking the question, while the second is the informal manner of asking it.

- If you were on the receiving end and was asked for your name, your answer must start with the phrase *Mi chiamo*...(mee *kyah*-moh), which stands for "My name is ..."

Answering with courtesy

- Saying "please" is helpful if you want other people to assist you. This phrase can be delivered in two ways: You can say *Per favore* (*pehr fah-voh-reh*) or *Per piacere* (*pehr pyah-cheh-reh*).

- Say "Thank You" by saying *grazie* (grah-tsee-eh).

- If you were the one who gave the favor to another person, it is also customary to say "You're welcome". This phrase can be delivered in Italian by saying either *prego* (*preh-goh*) or *non c'è di che* (*nohn cheh dee keh*).

- Did something wrong to another person? Then saying "I'm Sorry" or *mi dispiace* (*mee dees-pyah-cheh*) is necessary.

- If you want to be excused, say you need to go to the bathroom or answer a call, you say *mi scusi (mee skooh-zee)*. This is a formal way of saying "Excuse me."

- If you want to pass in the middle of people, the English expression "Excuse me" is also used. For Italians, though, the phrase *"permesso?"* (*pehr-mehs-soh*) is used. This can also mean "May I come in?" if you are at the door of somebody else's house.

- If you can answer another person's question by saying Yes or No, simply answer with *Sì* (sounds like the English word "see") or *No* (*noh*).

Conclusion

Thank you again for downloading this book!

I hope this book was able to help you learn more about how to speak Italian! Begin practicing today and in no time you will have the basics of Italian mastered!

Finally, if you enjoyed this book, please take the time to share your thoughts and post a review on Amazon. It'd be greatly appreciated!

Thank you and good luck!

Printed in Great Britain
by Amazon